chasing

your

mind

warrior

#38

MIND WARRIOR WOMAN —
CARRY OUR TORCH !

Chase Carey

chasing

TURN YOUR MIND

your

INTO A

mind

BLACK BELT'S MIND

warrior

C. CHASE CAREY, MBA
THIRD-DEGREE BLACK BELT

MOUNTAIN ARBOR
PRESS

MOUNTAIN ARBOR PRESS *an Imprint of BookLogix*

Alpharetta, GA

ISBN: 978-1-63183-574-2 - Paperback
eISBN: 978-1-63183-575-9 - ePub
eISBN: 978-1-63183-576-6 - mobi

Library of Congress Control Number: 2019938401

Printed in the United States of America   040119

♾ This paper meets the requirements of ANSI/NISO Z39.48-1992 (Permanence of Paper)

This book is dedicated to Lisa "Lisa Las Vegas" A. Carey, MBA, love of my life and best spouse ever! Without Lisa's never-ending support of me and my passions, none of my success would exist. Thank you, honey bunny!

It is never too late
to be the person you
always wanted to be.

—Paraphrase of George Eliot

CONTENT

FOREWORD

Jonathan Chapovsky, Fourth-Degree Black Belt
Chief Instructor, Karate Atlanta Martial Art Schools
Johns Creek, Georgia

W hat is a Black Belt leader, and how does one become one? Think and act like one.

Well, I will tell you, this is not an easy task. It is challenging to push yourself to your ultimate level of ability and mental state. And make no mistake, the biggest part is M-E-N-T-A-L. Understand that your growth is not only inevitable, but it comes with the humility to accept that we are not born superheroes. So far, the only naturally born superhero was Superman. The rest of us tapped into our unlimited potential to reach our goals. That's the seed we need to tap into so we can blossom into a Black Belt—or a Mind Warrior.

Will you choose to be a Mind Warrior?

I want to share with you my path to becoming a fourth-degree Black Belt and chief instructor in martial arts. But before I start, I want you to know that even though you may never step into a martial-arts studio before the day you die, **you *can* learn to think as I think, learn to act as I act, and learn to persevere as I persevere.** This will not make you a Black Belt, but it can make you a Mind Warrior, if you choose to learn. This is what I teach my students each and every day, from four- to five-year-olds, to adults in their thirties and forties, to adults in their fifties, sixties, seventies, and beyond.

I tell all of my students that Black Belts are never born Black Belts. We are never born as Mind Warriors, either. The issue is that many people—including myself when I started martial arts—are under the assumption that Black Belts were born as martial-arts savants and were so incredibly perfect they became instructors or higher-ranking Black Belts almost effortlessly.

This is not true! Martial-arts schools worldwide are filled with regular people with regular backgrounds who chose to become, well, "irregular." I experienced this firsthand. I started out as a funky, chubby, out-of-shape little boy who couldn't lift his leg to execute a kick to save my life. Exercise like running, push-ups, and other martial-arts training was very difficult for me and *out of the question*!

But, guess what? I was locked into training for a Black Belt thanks to my strong-willed, dedication-drilling, crazy mother that burned into me that quitting was *not* an option (Axioms 9 and 11). I started off enjoying classes, but that lasted about as long as my pinky finger. I trained because I had to, and once I came home, I forgot *all about* my uniform and martial arts. My instructors couldn't handle me because I was always the kid in the corner needing more help on my techniques and memorization of martial-arts forms, weapons routine, and the list goes on and on. The only thing I was semidecent at was flinging my fat hand into a board and breaking it. Other than that, not so good.

Could this have been any part of you at a time in life? It's not uncommon, but we can change. My change came from persistence, less thinking, and more doing. I didn't think about how hard my training was; I simply trained. And guess what? **Eventually, one day**

it all came together and I started to use my mind differently.

Why did I let people decide if I am good at something or not good at something?

Why did I limit myself and my skill mentally, emotionally, and physically?

Why was I going to let others assume I will not hit my goals?

Why can't I become a hero?

And that is where the future Black Belt was born (Axioms 1, 3, 8, 9). I simply had to choose not to let my as-yet-undisciplined mind tell me no. **It was my option what I wanted to think and do, and the moment I stopped letting my mind tell me I was a failure, I became a success.**

A concept that I teach my students is that "attitude drives behavior." This is a concept that I learned from my instructor to help us understand that the way we feel about our goals is going to influence the actions we take to reach them. **My attitude changed; therefore, so did my actions** (Axioms 3, 6). I started training harder. My goals got closer and closer. I was still fat, but that was not going to impede my level of success. My kicks went from fairly pathetic to almost straight up into the air (which is a really big thing).

Then guess what? My instructors started to notice my improved performance. I went from being the worst student on the training floor to the leader of the class. My strong will to become better was what drove me to do just that!

Finally, the day came to test for my first-degree Black Belt. I was *so* ready . . . or so I thought. I passed every test until I came face to face with the final one, which was the karate board break! **I couldn't break them; therefore, I was *not* awarded my Black Belt.**

My mentality of not being skilled at martial arts started creeping back in. **I started doubting myself again, and it was not until my instructor spoke to me very important words that reminded me that one test doesn't define one and one's skill; it is the strength of their heart and mind that breaks through unbelievable boundaries and levels.**

Summoning all that the broken pride and depression and changing my attitude once more, I finally earned my first Black Belt (see Axiom 9 again). Consider that a Black Belt is not an object. You'll never wear it to work or outside of martial-arts training and events. A Black Belt is actually **a presence** you bring to all around you. You can learn to become this presence by living the Axioms in this book. Yes, they work, and quite frankly, I was one of several instructors that taught them to the author over the years!

A Black Belt is simply a piece of cloth that is worn around the waist to hold up your pants—let's face it. The meaning, as you already know, does go much deeper. It is a physical representation of hard work, effort, dedication, and countless hours of sweat, pain, sometimes blood, and most importantly, perseverance. That's what this one piece of cloth represents. In fact, the first Black Belts were simply White Belts that had turned black after years of training, often in the dirt.

Martial-arts Black Belts are their very own breed of superheroes that influence such greatness in our society from day to day. Martial artists and Mind Warriors work countless hours to master the concepts of self-control and self-discipline, which makes them very powerful pillars in the world not just physically, but more importantly, through leadership, knowledge, and wisdom. **We help others to become the best version of them that they can be.**

This is what it means to be a Black Belt leader, or in your life, a Mind Warrior. It is not just the punching, and the kicking, and the board-breaking, and the flips, and the weapon tricks—*it is much more*. **It is way more about how you conduct yourself off the mat, outside of school, in the world. That is what being a Black Belt or Mind Warrior is all about.**

Make no mistake that it is also all about character. Everything we do is all about character.

Please join me in the journey to becoming a Mind Warrior.

**Mr. Brian Harrison,
Second-Degree Black Belt**

Consultant and Peer-Review Editor (and the man that constantly beats me at sparring!)

**Ms. Kristin Andree,
Second-Degree Black Belt**

Peer-Review Editor

ACKNOWLEDGMENTS

Thank you to my consultant and peer-review editors! Your keen insight and truthful improvements make this work so much better than it would have been otherwise.

Thank you to my copy editor, Rosemary Dreger of Copy Rose.

With much appreciation for so many wonderful people in my life, particularly my two favorite ladies: Lisa A. Carey, my wife, and Kaitlin T. Carey, my daughter. To my parents, William B. Carey Jr. and Elsie Louise Spatola Carey, both of whom sacrificed so much for the country and for their children.

Complete respect and honor to the ultimate Mind

Warrior, **Master Mark Alan Burns, sixth-degree Black Belt, four-time world champion.** Sir, you taught me to change my life *dramatically*, one class at a time, one struggle at a time, one kick at a time, one strike and block at a time, and one new understanding at a time. You encouraged me when I improved, and you picked me up when I fell down. To the people I grew up with, I am unrecognizable. To my daughter, I am a much better father. To my wife, I am a much better husband. To my clients, I am a much better professional, and to my friends, a much better friend. The six-plus years I was blessed to train under you are among the very most important of my life. My life can never be the same, and I will never forget this for one second. *This book is the direct result of just a fraction of the lessons and the enormous wisdom you taught me.* As you begin your next giant step at impacting the souls of this world, I say to you on behalf of the thousands you have already impacted so positively, *Tae Sa Bum Nim, Kam Sa Ham Me Da!* **"Master, thank you for teaching us!"**

Appreciation to my martial-arts teachers and fellow students: Ms. Teresa Azzarito, second-degree Black Belt; Mr. Jonathan Chapovsky, fourth-degree Black Belt, chief instructor; Ms. Dawn Wyatt Abercrombie, first-degree Black Belt; Mr. David Abercrombie, first-degree Black Belt; Ms. Kristin Smith Andree, second-degree Black Belt; Ms. Lina Arrango, first-degree Black Belt; Mr. Derrick Biellier, fourth-degree Black Belt; Ms. Hilary Boretz, second-degree Black Belt; Mr. Michael Briselden, second-degree Black Belt; Mr. Anthony Chalfant, first-degree Black Belt; Mr. Troy Dankworth, first-degree Black Belt; Mr. Brian Harrison, second-degree Black Belt; Mrs. Roseann Luberto Harrison, second-degree Black Belt; Ms. Linda Henninger, first-degree Black Belt; Mr. Steen Henninger, first-degree Black Belt; Mr. Eli Kafer, fifth-degree Black Belt; Mr. Jeff Leiby, first-degree Black Belt; Ms. Jennie Monahan, first-degree Black Belt; Mr. Curtis Montclair, Black Belt; Dr. Glendy Yeh Rappon, second-degree Black Belt; Mr. George Rauch, fourth-degree Black Belt; Mr. Juan Sotomayor, first-degree

Black Belt; Ms. Jessica Stokes, first-degree Black Belt; Mr. Greg Sword, first-degree Black Belt; Ms. Nicole Sword, first-degree Black Belt; Mr. Maxwell Van Eck, fourth-degree Black Belt, eight-time ESPN World Champion and eleven-time ATA World Champion; Ms. Aubrey Jordan Ward, second-degree Black Belt, RYT 500; Ms. Patti Cole White, first-degree Black Belt; Ms. Toni Wood, second-degree Black Belt, and Mr. Manual Yu, third-degree Black Belt.

Thank you to the owners of Karate Atlanta: Master Chong Sul, sixth-degree Black Belt; Master Craig Wolfel, sixth-degree Black Belt, and Mr. Chris Braba-zon, sixth-degree Black Belt. Special, honored thank-you to Grand Master Soon Ho Lee of ATA, who made my training and the training of tens of thousands of us possible.

To all those at the Monroe Institute and Hemi-Sync: AJ Honeycutt III, Nancy "Scooter" McMoneagle, Joe McMoneagle, Bob Monroe.

Remarkable people I consider my "dream team" in life: Renonda Anderson; Dawn Andrews; Rick Bailey; Vanessa Barigelli; Georgi Baldwin; Charlotte Baez-Diaz; Becca Bonacchi; Dr. Brad Bongiovanni; Professor James Borden, PhD, Villanova School of Business; Jack Brannigan; my brothers Jaime Carey, Judge Kevin J. Carey, JD, Esq., and the late Sean W. Carey, MD, PhD (who left us all too soon); Graham Cherrington; Connie Chesner; Kathy Cioffi; Rick Cohen; Dr. Stewart Colby, DVM; Travis Cook; Kimberly Cornelius; Jack Curtis, CEO of Corporate Health Partners; John "JD" Dammann, market vice president, wellness leader, Humana; Steve DeMoss; Ellen Diehl; Laura Dyett; Peg Eitl; Gayle Ely; Sheila Ewers, E-RYT 500, founder, Blue Lotus Yoga; Lisa Fetherolf; Glenn Frater; Annah Kate Gillette, CHC; Harvey Grady; Tara Goetz, MA, LPC; Kevin Grimes; Teresa de Grosbois; William Haight; Mia Hannah; Joe Harrison; Genna Harmon; Jennifer Heal, CFP; Henry Daniel Morrobel Hidago; Genevieve Hogan; Kerri Hummingbird; Brandell Inglis; the late Herb Kahl; Bryan Karetny; Reza

Khalaj; Brianna Nicole Kondos; Amanda Lavassani; Amber Cleveland Lewter, LPC, EdS; LaDonna Lewis; Asha Lightbearer; Kelley Linn; Amanda Llewellyn, producer, 4 L Films; Wes Llewellyn, 4 L Films; Jake Locklear, martial-arts student; Karen Malik, MA; Ted Malone; John Mamon; Ana Mancoci; Cathryn Marshall, MSA; Lauren Manners; Bill Marinella; Ted A. McCain; Rob Mello; Tony Milam, CPA, ABV; Elaine Mueller, RN, LMT; Sean Murphy, second-degree Black Belt; Gary Nichols; Sarah Nichols; Patty Nuzzo; John O'Brian, CFO/EVP Corporate Health Partners; Ivy Oxendine, JD; Dr. Joe Rappon, OD; Richard Pelay, leadership trainer; Catherine P. Perry, MEd, DD; Katheryn Plaza; Shirley Puccino; Mike Reeves; Brenda Rew; Denise Rhinehart, LMT; Mike Roddy; Ryan "Redhawk" Safoutin; Carol Sefers; Robert A. Spatola (my "Uncle Bobby," one of the most remarkable persons I've ever known); Dave Stachowiak; Courtney Stancil; Jim Somers; Dorothy Thomas; Jeff Tormey; Cailen Wells, DC.; Eddie S. Wilson III; Doug Yedinak (my barber from age fourteen to age thirty-eight); the

Canang YTTs (January–July 2018); and mentors Sonya Kuropatwa, E-RYT 500; Tami Roberts, RYT, LMT; Cybele Steen, E-RYT 500 and registered yoga therapist, and Aubrey Jordan Ward, second-degree Black Belt, RYT 500.

Each and every person named here has been—and many still are—a significant part of my life experience, and each has left a great impression with me. We can all be so much a positive part of each other's lives, even those we do not know, and even those we will never meet. These are among the best I know.

Mind Warriors choose to be a significant and positive influence in the lives of all others. We may have *no idea* the level of impact we may have on others, but we do so anyway . . . because we can. We are Mind Warriors.

INTRODUCTION

HOW TO READ THIS BOOK AND BECOME A MIND WARRIOR IN YOUR LIFE

Axiom is defined by *Merriam-Webster* as "a statement accepted as true as the basis for argument or inference: postulate sense (1) one of the axioms of the theory of evolution (2) an established rule or principle or a self-evident truth (3) a maxim widely accepted on its intrinsic merit."

In this book, we will define Axiom as all the above, but also as **a positive and disciplined point of view that creates the results that matter to me.**

The first thing you must know is that in this book, I am going to teach you how to develop a professional mind and to use it at a professional level of thinking. I am taking you beyond your childhood mind, beyond the mind you brought with you from school, beyond the adult mind you may only have.

The second thing you must know is that you have a Mind Warrior within you, and he, she, or it is dying to come out and to express more fully. No matter who you are, where you came from, or how you think, your Mind Warrior *is within you*. All you have to do to bring this aspect of yourself into the open is to be **willing to change the way you think and act**.

Brain scientists Andrew B. Newberg, MD, and Mark Robert Waldman have a book about neuroplasticity called *How God Changes Your Brain*. In their fascinating book, they explain how different areas of the brain can grow, retreat, and reform. I am certain my brain re-grew during my martial-arts training. Yours can, too.

At the age of fifty-four, I stepped into the Tae Kwon

Do studio near my home and signed up to get my Black Belt. What got me there was thirty-five years of interest and a not-so-good hospitalization two and a half months earlier. My goal was to get my Black Belt (first degree) so that I would no longer be taken advantage of in difficult situations. What I received was an unbelievable lesson in taking charge of my life.

Did I start off with a different education than the average person? Probably not. Did I start off better emotionally balanced than other people? Probably not. Physically more fit? Not a chance.

What I had to do to make the positive changes in my life that I needed was to train my brain to think differently, which caused me to feel differently, which enabled me to act in ways that supported my new desires and goals.

To do this, I took martial-arts training. I got lucky by training under a four-time world champion who ran a school less than a mile from my house: Master Mark Burns. But, what really got me to where I wanted to go was simply "showing up." ***That is the magic.*** Director and actor Woody Allen is quoted as saying, "Eighty percent of success is showing up." I think it's actually higher . . . much higher, in fact: somewhere between 95 percent and 98 percent.

In spiritual practices, which no doubt martial arts is, people like us who live normal lives not teaching spiritual practices are often referred to as "householders." You and me—friends on the weekend, perhaps sports for the kids, mow the lawn or water the plants, and maybe a bar-be-que; if we are lucky, a day at the beach, the lake, or in the mountains. Throughout the book I share simple stories from this perspective.

THE TAP SYSTEM

These Axioms are placed into three separate categories, which I call the **TAP System**:

T – Think: How Black Belts think differently

A – Act: How Black Belts act differently (often the result of thinking differently)

P – Perseverance: How Black Belts become Black Belts by "merely" persisting

You will find that the Axioms in these categories overlap and may fit in two or even three categories. They are segmented not to create an additional layer of understanding, but to encourage you to focus in just one dimension of the Axiom and perfect it before you expand its application. And indeed, there is often more than one dimension of application of any given Axiom.

INVITATION

My invitation to you is to choose not to be a "regular people," but rather to be an "irregular people." Stop driving fifty-five in the passing lane. Do something different. Do something in addition.

Step out of who other people told you to be, and be yourself. Be the best version of yourself. Go with what you think and what you feel. Be willing to let people not understand you. Forget that you have to be this or that, *particularly at what age*, to stretch yourself, to reach for something unusual, something special, something exciting, something really cool. It's not hard, just uncomfortable. (Okay, it is hard, too!) Be something really positive, exciting, and impactful. You can do that!

These Axioms are primarily from my experiences in martial-arts trainings, but also incorporate teachings from entrepreneurs, people in corporate America, professional athletes, actors, yogas and yoginis, leaders, parents, and the many, many bright and talented people I am so fortunate to work with.

I cannot say all of the Axioms come only from martial

arts, but I can say that I used each and every Axiom here to become a better version of myself. I use these Axioms as a sure-fire way to bend my reality to be much closer to what I deserve and want.

It is entirely possible that in giving credit for an Axiom to a specific person or training, I give credit to a person that was not the original idea generator. My intent is not to misstate origin, but to give respect to my many teachers.

Keep in mind that I in no way have all the answers to life. That said, I have had some rather interesting experiences and trainings while enduring many of life's most significant challenges such as death, severe illness, divorce, and job losses. (Remind me to tell you about the time I was fired three times from the same job at the same employer!)

I am certain that at least one of the many techniques that I have learned, applied, and share here will greatly benefit you or someone you know. And with that, I leave you to your training, young Black Belt Mind, in respect to you as you are and as you become.

Namaste.

C. Chase Carey, MBA, Third-Degree Black Belt, Yoga Teacher
The Palazzo, 31-700, Las Vegas, Nevada
Overlooking the Rock 'n' Roll Las Vegas Marathon and Half Marathon
November 11, 2018

T

HOW BLACK BELTS *think* DIFFERENTLY

Respect begins with this attitude: I acknowledge that you are a creature of extreme worth.

—Gary Chapman

Axiom 1: Always Start with Respect, *Always*

THE BACKGROUND

Mind Warriors always listen to others with full attention and respect, without judgment. In ATA Martial Arts, and many other traditions, we address each other with respect—always. The main outward view of doing this is by addressing each other as sir, mister, ma'am, missus, or miss, and the last name.

So, for example, if Mr. Harrison and I see each other at school (martial arts), it is "Hello, sir," or "Hello, Mr. Harrison." It is appropriate to address color belts by sir, mister, ma'am, missus, or miss, and their *first* name. But, once a Black Belt, it is required to address each other with sir, mister, ma'am, missus, or miss, and *last* name. All color belts must always address all Black Belts by their last name.

MY MESSAGE

When addressing another person in this respectful way, it automatically suppresses prejudgments on what the interaction will be. It sets aside any pent-up, knee-jerk, internal (often negative) reactions we may have. It creates a landscape of equality.

Pulling aside the knee-jerk reaction does not mean you have to bow down and be subservient to this other person; it simply means that every interaction you have will be on level ground. This other person might be your boss, or your boss's boss, your direct report, your parent, your spouse, or an in-law, and therefore, they have a different role, authority, or perspective than you might bring. You've still got to deal with mental and emotional equanimity in those situations, and you do that by starting with respect for them and for *you*.

Addressing each other with intentional respect reduces drama by automatically extending respect from you to the other person. Each and every person has their own story (or stories), and each and every person has their own series of experiences that got them to where they are or aren't. A remarkably few people get to adulthood (or very far through childhood) without very challenging circumstances. Showing respect for these experiences expresses to them that they earned the right to be who they are.

We show additional respect by actually listening fully to what the other person has to say, instead of just waiting for them to stop talking so we can speak. Listen with full attention, and when they have stopped speaking, pause and acknowledge you heard them. Then, if it's your turn, and *only* if it's your turn, speak.

YOUR ASSIGNMENT

Do try this at home, and do try this at work. At home, perhaps start with your spouse and children, and set an agreement to address each other as sir, mister, ma'am, missus, or miss, and their first or last name (whichever they choose). In the South, we have been doing this, regardless of martial-arts training, for over three hundred years. It is *very* effective. Have fun with it.

At work, start with your peer group. Say, "Hey, I just started this great book on a professional mind, and our first exercise is to address each other with respect for one week. Are you game?" No doubt, some will not be. Let them be. If everyone says no, then you simply address each person with respect, regardless of their position relative to you. If you start addressing everyone as sir, miss, etc., it will not be long before they are addressing you—and others—in the exact same way.

Write down your experiences and revisit what you wrote in two weeks' time.

Mind Warriors always listen to others with full attention and respect, without judgment.

Electric cars are not moving when they are being recharged. (Understand?)

Axiom 2: Meditate Daily and Live Mindfully

THE BACKGROUND

Mind Warriors know that everything is inside of us and spend significant time being there.

Meditate daily.

By now you've heard about meditation. You may already have a meditation discipline. You may even be a meditation expert. I hope so.

We can use your favorite search engine and find all the benefits of meditation. In 0.48 seconds, I got a return of 31,500,000 sites. But don't worry, as I am already halfway through them. Benefits include:

- Physical: Lower blood pressure, lower cortisol (stress hormone), the reactive parts of the brain shrink, and the creative areas of the brain expand. Remember neuroplasticity?

- Mental: Clearer thinking, clearer decision making, significantly reduced level of distracting thoughts.

- Emotional: Balance, ability to respond rather than react, improved use of emotions to support your life rather than them steering it. More sustained balance.

MY MESSAGE

Mindfulness is being present in the moment without judgment or anticipation. It means you gently focus on what is in front of you—a task at work, a conversation with a friend, playing with your child, or being in nature. *Now*, this very moment, is the only time that is real. Two seconds ago, two months ago, and twenty years ago are no longer real. Two seconds from now, two months from now, and twenty years from now are not yet real. There is a lot of scientific evidence that indicates what you are thinking and feeling now influences what will occur in your future: now, near, or far.

Mindfulness is the first 2 percent of meditation. But, it is just about the very most important 2 percent you can ever bring to your life.

Want to try a mindfulness exercise? Easy. Get up and go outside or to an enclosed atrium, take three three-part breaths (a bit deeper than your usual breath), and simply notice what you notice. If you get distracted, come back to your breath, then return to your environment. Do this for three to eight minutes to start.

What did you notice? In your next conversation, be

particularly mindful of being mindful. What do you notice? For many of us, it's that for the first time in our lives we were not pretending to listen just so we could say something back. We really listened.

Motivational speakers bank their lives on pulling you into the moment and creating a positive attitude and emotional feel and outlook in your life. And it works, but it doesn't last. Why?

Meditation is critical because it takes you not only to your subconscious mind, where permanent change is made, but also because it gives access to "all that is." (I think I got that from the film *The Legend of Bagger Vance*.) I mention motivational speaking because it doesn't reframe our subconscious mind, which means we don't take disciplined action with our conscious mind just a few hours after the motivational event. Meditation does.

Meditation is intelligently controlling your mind and

expanding its awareness and use of consciousness. We do meditation by:

1. Relaxing our bodies (so body inputs don't distract you)

2. Quieting our minds (so the mind chatter doesn't distract or add stress to you)

3. Moving into an expanded state of awareness (ESP)

ESPs are naturally occurring states, and you likely experience them frequently. If you are an athlete and have been in the "zone," that is an ESP. Have you ever had a lucid dream? That's an ESP. Have you ever had a great idea in the shower? That's an ESP. Do you have a significant prayer discipline? They often include ESPs. Have you ever had *great* sex? That's an ESP.

What happens when you meditate is this: a meditator's view of the distance between themselves and

God (divinity, universe, nature, source, etc.) diminishes significantly or goes away completely (Herbert Bensen, Harvard, 1970s). This is a permanent mind-changer, because meditation reprograms the subconscious mind.

Why? Because when you meditate, you move inside to the core of your being beyond many of the illusions and fears you (and me, too) face and deal with, including those we have no idea we are being affected by. (Remember the joke about the two fish? The one fish says to the other fish, "So, what do you think about all this water?" The second fish responds, "What's water?" Get it?)

Your connection with divinity (God, universe, nature, source, etc.) is not above you or outside of you; it is inside of you. It has always been there and always will be. When you are connected with divinity, you are connected to *all* things. When you realize you are connected to all things, you understand that you have direct access to all of the resources in the world. When you understand that connection—that access—you lose your fear of loss, and you lose your belief that "that person" is not you. You begin to understand the world more clearly: that we are all connected, including being connected to animals, insects, creatures, and forms of life as well as human.

Your mind, your heart, and your actions move away from "separateness" to compassion, cooperation, and inclusion. Your consciousness rises, which makes it easier for the consciousness of others to rise. When consciousness rises, the new things we do don't create other problems along the way.

Just as importantly, but beyond the scope of this book, is that in meditation you can develop direct access to your subconscious mind, where all resistances and fears hide out. Release them, and you will experience complete and total freedom. This is what a yogi is referring to when he or she refers to a state of Samadhi.

Samadhi is when you no longer perceive a barrier between what you see as yourself and all other things.

In fact, advanced meditators begin to understand there is only one "thing," which is *everything* as one whole. (Yes, this is pretty deep.) This understanding takes time and may take several lifetimes. (See *Chasin' Meditation* Chapter 9 for advanced techniques to dialogue with your subconscious mind.)

YOUR ASSIGNMENT

Meditate regularly.

Notice I didn't say daily. Why? Because most of us who develop a regular discipline of meditating frequently will get to the place where we will crave a daily meditation. So, I am not worried.

Okay, a few pointers about meditation:

- The best time to meditate is the time that works best for you. That said, if you can meditate in the morning, that can help the day to go better. (Disclosure: I tend to meditate at night or in the afternoon. I'm busy, just like you. But, I do miss my morning meditations.)

- Work up to meditating for twenty minutes twice a day. There is good science around this. That said, I prefer to meditate once a day for about thirty to forty-five minutes.

- Meditate in a special place—an extra bedroom, a corner of your den, or living room. Place something nice there to "set the stage." I like antiques and Kansas, so I have a part of a fossilized bison jaw from Kansas on a mouse-chewed antique feed bin. They make me feel at home.

- Background music (without words) can help keep your mind quiet and your body relaxed.

- Silent mantras can be very helpful in keeping distracting thoughts at bay.

- Hemi-sync (binaural beat) or SAM technology is remarkably helpful. Spend the twenty dollars and download a few meditations from The Monroe Institute (where I learned to meditate). They are now licensed to the company Hemi-Sync (www.Hemi-Sync.com).

Have you ever noticed that cars—gas or electric—are not moving when they are being refilled or recharged? Your mind, body, and spirit work the same.

Write down your experiences and revisit what you wrote in two weeks' time.

Mind Warriors know that everything is inside of us. We spend significant time being there.

Axiom 3: Yes, You Can! If You Say You Can or Say You Can't, You're Right

THE BACKGROUND

Mind Warriors know whether we think we can or we can't, we're going to be right. Yes, you can!

Whenever a martial artist goes to practice breaking boards in class, they first tap their chest with their right hand and firmly belt out, "Yes, I CAN!" Then, *bam*! The board is crushed. I cannot explain exactly how yelling (we call it a "kihap") increases our power, but it does.

Part of the answer is likely that the yelling blocks out all other thoughts (particularly the fearful "I can't" thoughts) and helps us to project our energy forward.

This does create great confidence, which is a major achiever, as well. (I am sure physiologists can explain the "why" in much better detail.)

When I coach women in self-defense, the most important thing I teach them, regardless of their physical capabilities, is this: when attacked, don't be afraid. Get angry and *stay* angry. When you are angry, fear vanishes. Anger comes solely from the belief that you or someone you care for has been severely wronged. When a person feels severely wronged, they will do almost anything to correct the bad.

MY MESSAGE

The "Yes, I can!" portion is also, I believe, a forceful exercise of will, which is one of the most powerful creative forces available to humankind (see Axiom 15). Don't think so? Do any of you have, or have had, a small child that does not want to be picked up? He or she will cross their arms, hold them tightly to their

Alex Rogan: Listen, Centauri, I'm not any of those guys. I'm a kid from a trailer park.

Centauri: If that's what you think, then that's all you'll ever be!

—*The Last Starfighter*

chest, and stare you down like a wild ox. And, they get heavier! I swear to God, they get heavier. Many of us have experienced this. How is this possible?

Henry Ford is quoted as saying, "Whether you think you can, or if you think you can't—you're right."

Where we tend to get hung up in applying this is in two places. The first is often with those people with difficult pasts. These people often, but not always, tend to believe they are not good enough or deserving enough to succeed in a big accomplishment. The second is timing of the result. Let's talk about the first one first, because that is simpler to clear.

When a person has self-doubt due to lack of belief of being good enough or deserving enough, the origin of that comes from a distorted (e.g. incorrect) belief due from a past—real or imagined—circumstance. That can be readily removed through competent therapy (which is a serious mechanism for spiritual growth) or through meditative healing practices (there is some of that in my book *Chasin' Meditation*, but you'd have to look for it).

The second is the real killer. There are over seven billion people on the planet. There is a very wide gap between those with natural-born talent to those with nearly no talent. Those with nearly no talent are almost always those relatively young in their incarnations. They are not going to be a Tony Robbins or Elon Musk in this lifetime or in the next two hundred. And there are those on the other end of the spectrum, the Tony Robbinses and Elon Musks, who combine incredible born-with mastership and very hard work to make their life look, well, like magic. The rest of us are in the great vast middle.

That said, many of us in this vast middle land can become much more Tony Robbins–like and Elon Musk–like in our lifetimes by learning to think like Black Belts think. Some say I am mistaken, and that regular people cannot become irregular people in just one lifetime, but I've seen this disproven way too many times to believe it.

My point being, the rest of us need to work at creating what we previously, and erroneously, believed we couldn't. It takes time, and it takes exertion of will. A good friend of mine, "Janet," just ran for her first political office, a house seat in Georgia, and lost. It's not a surprise she lost; the odds were against her. She ran against a well-seated, long-time incumbent who has a strong, positive reputation and who used his influence to convince voters she stole from her campaign and was not a person of integrity. Did she expect to win? Yes, she did! She really did, and she put in the fundraising and work to make it happen. But, there was a "bad" person who did bad things, and that helped keep her out of office (that time, that election, that day).

But is she thinking, *No, I can't*? Not at all. She knows, not thinks, that this was simply the first step to achieving her goals in politics, whatever they may be.

So, as a result of these and many other influences, we say "I can't!" instead of "I can't *yet.*" We tend to answer these questions too literally. When most people ask you whether or not you can do something, they are asking not if you can or can't do that particular thing, but rather asking if you can or could do that particular thing. There is a very big difference between these two. HUGE! (Thank you, movie *Pretty Woman!*)

Often, the greatest changes in perception can occur with just a slight twist of the main way of thinking. I saw two news commentators talking about something we, the United States, had done rather poorly (understatement). The one commentator said, "Well, the one thing we learned is not to do that again." George Will, the other commentator said, "No, the one thing we learned is not to do that thing *that way* again." Incredible difference with just the very slightest change in perspective.

In a recent workshop, I was teaching mindfulness and meditation techniques for performance and stress management (and for other results, too). When I went around the room to ask for volunteers as to what stressed them most at work, one gentleman named Timothy said that each and every day he would be presented with a problem he had never solved before, and they were *big* problems with *big* impacts. (Timothy works for a major construction company that works on enormous physical objects.) The first thing I asked him was whether he had ever been presented with a problem he could not fix. "No" was his simple answer. Because of his Mind Warrior focus on results, he was known as the company's guru, a title he had earned with a lot of hard and impressive work.

So, the next time you are asked "Can you do this thing?" first think about whether you can. And if you can't, in that very moment ask yourself what you *could do* to figure it out. Your new Mind Warrior response may then be "I can't at this exact moment, but I will have an answer for you in X amount of time."

That response, ladies and gentlemen, is worth all the tea in China. Your leadership team at work will take notice, and you will be catapulted to a whole new level of understood contribution. You will be the new company guru! (Not a bad gig, if you can get it.)

YOUR ASSIGNMENT

I want you to "Yes, I can!" something, and then do it. If it does not result in success the first time, do the "Blah, blah, blah . . . and REPEAT!" thing.

How many of you got the very first job you applied for? Is the first person you dated your spouse? Did you have a child the very first time you tried? (That's the *one* thing no one seems to mind repeating: the trying part!) Did you get that promotion the first time you went for it? Did you get an A on your very first exam?

If you said yes to all these things and more, then you don't need to keep reading this book. But, if you are like most of us Mind Warriors in training, let's keep going.

Write down your experiences and revisit what you wrote in two weeks' time.

Mind Warriors know whether we think we can or we can't, we're going to be right.

Axiom 4: Limit the Access People Have to You and Your Time

THE BACKGROUND

Mind Warriors know the most important thing they can put into their mind is nothing. You probably have no idea how much of your attention you give away to others each and every day. Sometimes when you do this, it makes sense: paying attention getting to work, responding to your boss and co-workers, ordering lunch, taking care of your children, working out, and hanging with your friends.

But, most of what we pay attention to is of no value to us. In fact, the scary thing is, much of this nonvalue information is to our detriment: buy this; buy that;

eggs are bad for you; no, wait, they're actually good for you; eat animals; don't eat animals; this political party is ruining your life; no, wait, it's the other party; sorry, our bad, and there are no other parties than the two biggies; GMOs; global warming; illegal immigration; health care; more prescription drugs; more poison for our lawns, which drains off into your community's water system; let's start another war; no, let's not, but let's spend the money anyway; the country doesn't have the money to do this or that, but all of a sudden it has the same amount of money for something else; we don't have enough money for infrastructure repairs; aliens are real; UFOs are manmade; use sunscreen before you go out into the sun; but wait, the sunscreen is bad for the environment; what, you don't have the latest, greatest cell phone? Don't buy the one your parents use; after all, they are adults, and what do they know? And god only knows what else . . .

The above points of view I pulled from just *this week's* news stories, and it's only Wednesday! Here's a very important point: **you do not need to have an opinion about everything everyone wants you to have an opinion about.**

Many times, people looking for your pointed point of view are simply looking for reinforcement about their pointed point of view, or to start a fight about your skewed point of view. It is perfectly acceptable to say when pushed, "I am not sure what I think about that." Some will push you further and insist, in order to be a good person, you *must* have a pointed opinion. Simply respond by saying, "I understand your concern—it is a valid one. I am working hard to make a life for myself and my family, learn more, stay current, and be responsible. I am simply not as informed on this subject as you appear to be." That's all. This is a perfect use of Axiom 1: Always Start With Respect, Always.

MY MESSAGE

Your subconscious mind is always active and fully

Stop! There's so much noise in here I can't even hear myself think!

—Every parent on the planet

engaged. Whether or not you *notice* an external piece of information has zero effect on whether or not you retain it. Your subconscious mind is absorbing it all in three dimensions, high definition, with complete integrity. If you pass a billboard for a particular soft drink, completely don't notice it, then happen to stop for lunch, and the advertised soda (which is not your go-to drink) is offered, the chances you will buy the advertised beverage rather than your go-to is quite a bit higher. Quite a bit. Advertisers know this.

This happens with everything we or others think, say, and do. **The more emotion attached to the external information, the more it sticks in the front of our subconscious mind.**

Ever notice that many alcohol commercials show young men in a room full of very pretty women, or just one guy with two or more women on a beach? Accident? Not a chance. Ever notice that products targeted to women almost always include other women (put it out of your mind, guys . . .) and are more likely to include pets?

Did you know the fact that you are reading this book increases the likelihood that you will take martial-arts lessons? Kind of scary, right?

Jim Borden, an assistant professor at Villanova University, has a footer in his email that quotes Jim Rohn: ***"The difference between where you are today and where you'll be five years from now will be found in the quality of books you've read."*** Isn't this the absolute truth?

Do you know the phrase "Garbage in, garbage out"?

YOUR ASSIGNMENT

This one is easy. I want you to do *less*.

The suggestion is going to involve your cell phone, so

I am only going to suggest this exercise be done after checking with your doctor, and only for two days. Let your local ER know you are going to do this, just in case it gets to too hard and you stroke out. Reach out to all your emergency contacts and warn them. Tell your children you love them but may never see them again.

After you get home from work, maybe even *at work*, when your cell phone rings, vibrates, beeps, plays Beethoven's Symphony No. 9, don't answer it, and don't look at it. Yes, I *actually said that*, and in writing, too! (For those of you that just had a chill run up your spine, you're in real trouble. You're in deep, but don't despair. There's still a chance to save you.)

You are going to find this hard to believe, but after work I place my cell phone on my kitchen counter (which is central in my evening activities) or place it in the sunroom, which is where my wife and I hang out. It is not in my hand, often not within reach, and almost always when it makes a noise, unless it is the ringtone associated with my daughter, I ignore it. Sometimes this drives my wife crazy—absolutely nuts.

In fact, the fitness device on her wrist notifies her of emails, texts, phone calls, and occasionally fitness things. That drives me crazy. If it's *that* important, they will call, text, or *whatever* me again and again, or reach out to my wife, who is sure to pay attention. But, that doesn't mean I have to!

Think about it. Unless you are an ER physician, on call for work, are a first responder, in the military, or have children outside of your home, there just isn't anything that is *that important*. Plus, Publisher's Clearing House always knocks on your door with a camera crew; they do not collect phone numbers! I know, many of us think its "dope" to be so tuned into our telephones, but they just really make us dopes.

Did you ever see the ad of a dog smoking a cigarette? An ad of someone walking down the street holding their cell phone out in front of them looks just as ridiculous. The only possible value in someone walking down the street holding a cell phone out in front of them would be to cull the herd. Unfortunately, the culling isn't happening fast enough!

Write down your experiences and revisit what you wrote in two weeks' time.

Mind Warriors know the most important thing we can put into our mind is *nothing*.

All successful people are comfortable with being uncomfortable.

—Wise saying known throughout entertainment, business, and athletics

Axiom 5: Work-Home-Life Balance Is a Myth— Get over It!

THE BACKGROUND

Mind Warriors know that life is really a dance of beautiful moments and routine moves with the occasional slip and fall. And we love every moment of it. Suck it up, buttercup, and get over it!

The fact is, you don't *want* to be balanced. When you are balanced, nothing you are doing is moving. When something is not moving, there is *zero inertia* going on. Maybe we need to get some background in classical physics. Inertia tells us that a body in motion continues to stay in motion, and a body at rest continues to stay at rest. Is it easier to get up from two hours in an easy chair or get up from five minutes of doing push-ups? Push-ups, right?

A few years ago, a buddy and I went skiing in Colorado with the Atlanta Ski Club. I always took lessons when I skied for a week, and was pleased when my buddy bought a ski-lesson DVD. We would watch it endlessly at night and practice it all day. From the two hours of DVD, I practiced mostly the very first lesson. **In that lesson, the instructor said most people who fall while skiing lose their balance when one ski is knocked off the snow, which happens all the time. His answer? It wasn't to only ski where there was flat terrain; it was to learn to ski on just one ski—whichever one stayed on the ground.**

I started lifting my right ski two inches off the snow in a relatively flat area for three seconds, and eventually worked my way up to downhill for almost thirty seconds with a ski lifted. The result was that within just a few days, I was skiing double-black-diamond slopes.

(Yes, my heart was beating its way out of my chest, but I didn't fall!)

Skiing is a great analogy for moving through life. Yes, the flat parts are nice because of the snow and the fresh air, but the real excitement comes with steeper, ever-changing terrain. This book will help you to embrace life as it presents itself, particularly when one foot is not on the ground.

Let's expand on balance. When you study the orbits of electrons around an atom's nucleus, you discover that the electrons don't form the fancy shells fully encasing the nucleus that are often depicted. The shells are a *representation* of all places any given electron may be at any given moment in time. The reality is that at any given moment in time, an electron is, say, here, and the nucleus is way over there, and then a split moment later, the electron is way over there and the nucleus is relatively right here. Consider this. If I did my math correctly, the nucleus of a hydrogen atom is two thousand times the mass of its own orbiting electron. Now, imagine if your left butt cheek was two thousand times the mass of your right butt cheek. You'd have a hell of a balance problem! But over time, you'd figure it out.

MY MESSAGE

At any given moment in your life, with very, very few exceptions, you are out of balance. We often label such moments perceived as negative as being off balance, and when perceived as positive, in the groove. That's the way life works. If you have sharp perceptions of being off balance or in the groove, take a longer look—a much longer look.

In martial arts, particularly in sparring (regulated fighting), to make a strike or block, *we have to go from a moment of complete balance to a moment of no balance*. We always use a reciprocal action to counter the imbalance.

For example, if we strike a punch with our right fist (it's not all karate chopping), we counterbalance that action by pulling back on our left arm just as quickly and with just as much force. So, if your life feels largely unbalanced negatively, stop and add positive experiences.

Another skill taught is to put our attention (primarily eyes) directly on our target (the person we are sparring) and not look all around. When you are looking all around, you open yourself up to taking a sharp and painful strike. We always look at our target. This behavior has a direct effect off the mat, as well. When we start—you and me, us householders—to look around at things around us, we will always find things that appear easier or better for others, and that alone makes us feel off balance. If we use this same experience of viewing others to help us do things in better ways in our lives, that is a positive application of attention. If we use the experience of others to help us feel bad, inadequate, unappreciated, we are participating in a negative application of attention. Don't do that.

So, the real skill to learn here is existing on the edge, seemingly in balance. You want to have the feel of balance, but you want to be able to pounce at the next different thing, do it, and reset without falling down or losing concentration.

The more you move through life as a dance, the smoother it will be. Yes, significant challenges can and likely will arise; they do to all of us. When you resist a situation simply because something is not as you wish it, you add sharp edges to the event, and you get cut when you might otherwise have just been bruised.

Don't get me wrong. My challenges are not necessarily anything I enjoy, particularly when they are the complete opposite of what I am wanting, and I have resisted them. Yes, I've gotten mad, angry, frustrated, stupefied at the intensely selfish actions of others. I've gone out on my front porch and yelled at God, telling Him how bad He is at His job. (The front porch has a metal roof, so that was probably not the smartest thing to do!)

That said, it made me feel a lot better. It also would rattle my body for as much as a couple of hours, so even in the short run, it was a very inefficient response to the negative stimuli. For some time now, when I get into a stressful challenge, I think about the status of the things that really matter to me. Do I have a good relationship with my wife and daughter? Yes. Do I have a comfortable place to live? Yes. Do I have opportunity? Yes. Throw a great family dog on top of it, and I have a pretty good life, and I find great gratitude in that.

(Hint: Expressing genuine gratitude releases a lot of resistance, letting life events smoothly go by.)

YOUR ASSIGNMENT

Most all actions require change: set (getting your balance), execute, reset, and then repeat. Take a look at three recent weeks in your life in this order:

1. A week that was out of control and you didn't get to do what you wanted to do at all

2. A week that was a mix of out of control and in control

3. A week that went just beautifully, and you got to do everything you wanted to do

Now, spend some time with a tablet and write down all the things in your life that got destroyed by week one. With the few exceptions of extreme hardship, the list is likely very short or nonexistent.

If you missed one of your kid's soccer practices or games, don't write that down. The kids are fine and need to learn to deal with a world that is no longer 1950s America. If your spouse got really upset with you, don't write that down. He or she is likely to get upset every now and then, and you've just gotten the bad time over with. If you had a car accident where no one was hurt and the insurance company paid for most of it, don't write that down. If your boss was jerking you around and you didn't respond effectively, don't write that down, either.

Are you getting my point? Have you picked up yet that balance is also determined by your perspective? Two identical people standing side by side may have completely different outlooks on what balance is for them.

Did you ever read about the one pair of Siamese twins that got sick differently? One could have a cold, and the other could be completely healthy, even though they shared the same blood!

Okay, back to your assignment.

The next thing I want you to do is to get into meditation and ask your inner being (which is your subconscious mind) why having a "bad" week was so challenging for you. Ask this part of you what it is afraid of.

In the short run, balance is a myth. It only works in the long run. A real goal is to find balance in unbalance, grasshopper.

Write down your experiences and revisit what you wrote in two weeks' time.

Mind Warriors know that life is really a dance of beautiful moments and routine moves with the occasional slip and fall. And we love every moment of it.

A

HOW BLACK BELTS *act* DIFFERENTLY

The world moves positively through the intelligent action of good people doing great things.

Axiom 6: Exchange, Not Sacrifice

THE BACKGROUND

Mind Warriors invest in their physical, mental, emotional, and spiritual health in disciplined routines. What do martial artists sacrifice when they sign up for training? *Nothing.* Not . . . a . . . thing! They simply *exchange* one thing for another. They exchange activities (or nonactivities) for a beneficial discipline of activities that is not only great for them, but exciting, challenging, and exhausting, too.

"Yes, but practice can be three to four times a week, plus private trainings, special workshops, testings, and tournaments," I hear you say. Well, let's see. I say,

I did give up drinking beer and watching TV for the forty-five minutes during which I was in class, or perhaps just vegging, or working later than I needed to or was beneficial for anyone. I consider that a good trade. (Any *Dances with Wolves* fans out there?)

When I did sign up for training, I had to make the decision committing to the work and struggle to be a Black Belt ahead of everything else in my life other than my wife and daughter. I did work fewer hours, and my business probably did not grow as fast as it could have, but my business did do well. I spent less time with friends, but did find new friends. I did have to exchange more routine dinners with my wife (trainings are mostly in the evening, and you cannot eat beforehand) for more date-night dinners, something she and I love more.

A note for parents: My daughter did not grow up with me, and that allowed my nonassigned time to be freer, so I do feel for you there. *That said*, a lot of adults I train with also have their children enrolled. My martial-arts friends Mr. Brian Harrison and Mrs. Roseann Harrison have a grand total of five Black Belts in their family, all having trained together. Doing so actually increased the time their family spent together.

MY MESSAGE

Is being physically, mentally, emotionally, and spiritually fit a sacrifice? I don't think so. My physical, mental, emotional, and spiritual health are quantum leaps better than when I started my training, and my daughter feels much better that her dad is doing something to stay healthy. In fact, while writing this, I am enrolled in yoga-teacher training and hope to be a certified yoga teacher soon, none of which would have happened if I had not trained for my Black Belt. (I did recently receive my certification.) Plus, there is an added benefit: my daughter, Kaitlin, is a new, yet avid, yoga student. This gives dad and daughter a significant opportunity for years of great shared experiences.

YOUR ASSIGNMENT

Ask two people that know you well if they see you not doing something beneficial because you are not wanting to sacrifice. Be open and thank them. Then, in your meditation practice (Axiom 2), see if they are right.

Do not beat yourself up. Simply explore to see if you can recognize any of this going on with you, and see what you are willing to exchange in your life—even if just with your little toe—to move forward in an area that would benefit you.

Write down your experiences and revisit what you wrote in two weeks' time.

Mind Warriors invest in their physical, mental, emotional, and spiritual health in disciplined routines.

Axiom 7: If You Cannot Kick to the Head, Kick to the Stomach

THE BACKGROUND

Mind Warriors are so good at even just one thing, they cannot be ignored.

In my college years, my mom gifted me with a leather wall hanging of the poem "Desiderata" by Max Ehrmann. In part, it says, "If you compare yourself with others, you may become vain and bitter, for always there will be greater and lesser persons than yourself. Enjoy your achievements as well as your plans. " a.k.a., play to your strengths!

Now, if you want to get better in some aspect of your

life, by all means, train and practice, train and practice, train and practice. But, also understand the limits you may have. As a martial artist, I will not likely ever kick above my belt level (which is the very minimum height required). Could I get there plus one inch? I probably could, but it would take a lot of sustained work and be quite painful because of the way my hip joints are oriented (and everyone's are different). It's not a muscle limitation for me; it a skeletal-structure limitation.

But hear this: in competition, a perfectly placed, low side kick will score higher over a less perfectly placed, high side kick every day of the week.

. . . But, make it the *very best kick anyone has ever seen*!

MY MESSAGE

Bruce Lee, one of the most remarkable athletes and martial artists in recorded history, is quoted as saying (paraphrase), "I fear not the man who practiced ten thousand

How do you get to Carnegie Hall? Practice, man, practice.

—*Old parable*

kicks once each, but the man who has practiced one kick ten thousand times." So, if you want to look like the best martial artist in the world, pick ten thousand different kicks and strikes, and practice them once. There will be a lot of work for you in Hollywood and in life.

But, if you want to crush real life, practice your one kick (front, side, round, hook, etc.) or strike ten thousand times, and you will be unbeatable. You will be so good that, as Steve Martin has said, "They can't ignore you." How would you like that on your résumé? "The person who is so good, she just can't be ignored!"

After a short while, your reputation will precede you, so you won't need a résumé at all. That's a pretty solid deal.

YOUR ASSIGNMENT

I cannot say I want you to go out and practice your side kick ten thousand times (you've figured by now that's my favorite kick), but I do want you to look at several aspects of your life, pick one, and then do a drill down to see what parts you can master.

Want to be a better leader at work or in the community? Great! Want to be a better spouse or parent? Perfect! Want to be a better neighbor or coworker? Wonderful!

As an example, I have a friend, Cat Marshall, who is a personal trainer and speaker. She is known in North Metro Atlanta as the best friend ever! Everybody wants Cat to be their friend. Why? Because she always has something remarkably positive to say to you, and then shares it with everyone she knows; sends very nice "thinking of you" gifts to her lady friends for no reason (as a guy, such things don't do much for me, but they do for ladies), and then once a year, she gets everyone she knows together for dinner at a great restaurant. She makes us all feel valued and important. Folks, that's a skill we can all benefit from.

But, what if you are not a big social-skills person?

When I was first in the corporate world working as a group insurance underwriter, I was a pretty technical employee, although I had a good personality, too. I found the technical aspects of the work fascinating. I intensely read every technical memo and email that came out, and catalogued them in a very large set of files. So, when those odd but important "one-off" circumstances came around, I was the go-to underwriter; they were a breeze for me. Everyone, and I mean everyone, knew I had the answers, and my coworkers really appreciated my ability to produce hardly known fixes to uncommon but important work challenges. So, for me, that was my side kick.

How did I do it? I picked "one thing" (remember that from *City Slickers*?), and I practiced it until it became part of me and my muscle memory (including brain muscle) was set in stone. Then I went on to two other areas and kept it at that. I did *not* try to be all things to all people, because I recognized at a young age that I could not be. And that was not my strength.

More homework: Pick something you would really like to be good at (or knowledgeable at) and read five pages a week for a year, or practice it for forty-five minutes a week for a year. It's not so important what you pick as how you will view yourself differently after fifty-two weeks, and how the people around you will view you differently.

Write down your experiences and revisit what you wrote in two weeks' time.

Mind Warriors are so good at even just one thing, we *cannot* be ignored.

Don't be addicted to approval. If you can't break the habit, get a dog

—Dawn Andrews

Axiom 8: Don't Practice until You Get It Right— Practice until You Can't Get It Wrong

THE BACKGROUND

Mind Warriors know their techniques on a level that would make a US Navy Seal squeal. Okay, maybe not that extreme, but close. You and I, through school exams and deadlines at work, were taught to study, practice, and train until we got it right. That makes a lot of sense. Would it make sense to practice or study until we *almost* get it right? Well, if you approach what you do as a C student, then maybe it would. But for a lot of people, we want to be good at what we do. So, we practice until we get it right, because then we can pass the exam, do the chore for Mom and Dad, or get that project done at work.

MY MESSAGE

This approach is very efficient if there is a clear, non-changing test or deliverable. It enables us to deploy resources, including our time and thinking, to produce the result we want. But what if the test or the event turns out to be something we did not expect? In two words, we're screwed. Why? Because we didn't study, practice, or train so well that we could navigate into the result from a different direction.

Have you ever taught a course, a class, or given a lecture on a topic that was complex? And if so, did you ever give one of these classes without any significant preparation? If so, you know the difference between practicing until you get it right versus practicing until you can't get it wrong. It's really the difference between seeing something in a two-dimensional photo versus a 3D, HD model.

If you want to outperform others, first outperform yourself.

The US Navy SEALs do this. If you read the story about when the SEALs stormed Bin Laden's compound, you will see the perfect example of this Axiom. They had a perfect full-size model of the entire compound built. Then they devised a plan and practiced that plan by storming the duplicate compound. They did this again and again until they got it right.

Then, they boarded their helicopters and flew to Pakistan, right? No, not right! What they did next was intentionally alter doorways, hallways, rooms, etc. and executed their plan, figuring out the best way to respond to the unexpected change. And then they practiced this scenario again, and again, and again.

Then what? No, not the helicopter yet. They then changed other structures, then simulated equipment failure, simulated SEALs being killed or wounded, simulated being discovered. Yes, again, and again, and again.

YOUR ASSIGNMENT

The difference in the amount of training it takes between these two levels of skill is about 2 percent to 50 percent. The difference in these two levels of delivery is about 250 percent. This is how I won a district championship in martial-arts weapons. During the tournament, when I performed my weapons form, I made a mistake: I didn't execute a move perfectly, but I got a very good score anyway. Then, another competitor had his turn and he made no mistakes. His form was not as hard or interesting as mine, but it was performed flawlessly, and it was one that took incredible practice. Solid quality and solid performance. We ended up tying.

But, as in many things in life, ties are not permitted. And of course, we were competing.

We each had to go again. This is a brutal, stressful, and difficult thing to do, and the difficultly is almost always only in our minds.

Well, I knew my form so well, I did not have to think about the order of moves (there were likely forty-five to fifty) or how to execute them. Because of this, I was able to focus 100 percent on improving each of my moves, particularly the one I did not do well the first time.

Yes, I won that competition.

How could I do this? I trained until I knew the material, in effect, in 3D.

Your homework is to look at work, at your place of worship, in your community, take on something you have been doing a bit better than well, or take on a new task that has to be taught to others, and learn it like you have never learned anything before. And then teach it. You will see the difference on the faces of your students. Trust me.

Write down your experiences and revisit what you wrote in two weeks' time.

Mind Warriors know our techniques on a level that would make a US Navy Seal squeal. (Okay, maybe not that extreme, but close!)

Axiom 9: If You Fall Down Seven Times, Get Up Eight

THE BACKGROUND

Mind Warriors *always* get back up and keep fighting, because that's what we do. I am not sure that math really works out right here, but it's a great Axiom. I can tell you it was taught to me by a powerful teacher, Aubrey Jorden Ward, and I can tell you just how powerful this is. This expression has been around a long time, and it is a keeper, and there is a very good reason for that. This is experienced in life in martial arts, yoga, parenting, being a leader/manager/boss, friend, peer, neighbor, and everything and anyone else in life. And it can apply to everything.

Those who [are] mastered in the art of falling have no fear of rising!

—Mehmet Murat Ildan

Keep in mind that the only people who fail are those that quit. It is not those who tried and didn't win.

There might be something innate in me about fighting back—perhaps a self-survival skill. When I would get beat up or pushed around as a kid, which was not often, I did always get right back up and stand my ground, even if I didn't have a *chance* against the other person! Was I scared doing this? At times, for sure. You bet. But I did it, and they backed off.

MY MESSAGE

The last person standing is always the winner, but you may get there much sooner than eight tries. It's the attitude that makes you win. If you get back up, you're back in the fight and you haven't lost. Play tennis? Ever get your butt kicked—kicked hard? Yeah, me, too. But you get back on the court. Ever get mistreated at work? Did you stand up for yourself, or learn to stand up for yourself? Yeah, me, too. Uncomfortable . . . yeah, it can be really uncomfortable. But, few things feel as good as standing up for yourself, and it works!

I had a pretty good job at one company, and for a while I had a pretty hard-hitting boss who was also a pretty low performer, which made things even harder because he could not tell what the right things to do were. He put mechanisms in place to keep me in my place. I was scared and I did not fight back. And then one day, it was just too much and I bit back, didn't even think about it, didn't even take time to sharpen my teeth. I just bit. It was a damn good bite, and I walked away with a pretty good chunk of him. So, he started giving other people his bark, but he never barked at me again.

Can you think of a great sports figure or a politician that got hit hard, but got right back into the game? Sure, you can. They are easy to name.

Lee Iacocca, an old name in business, ran the creation of the Mustang for the Ford Motor Company, an American icon that will live on forever. And then Lee Iacocca got fired and kind of screwed in the termination, so his book says. But, he licked his wounds, dusted himself off, and got a job at Chrysler Motor Corporation—not everyone's first pick. Well, he did many things there, including bringing back the first production of an American convertible since the 1976 Cadillac El Dorado, and introduced suburban moms and dads to this new thing called a minivan.

Anyone out there ever been divorced? It doesn't matter which side of the fence you were on in one of those; they are brutal, particularly if children are involved. They say the best divorce is when both spouses feel they were screwed in the process. True or not true, I cannot say, but interestingly enough, in the area where I live, people will literally spend hundreds of thousands of dollars and years to get absolutely as much as they can in a divorce or to inflict as much pain as possible.

This is all ego-driven, and it keeps many people from getting up that eighth time.

Did I mention the time I was fired three times from a consulting gig? I was doing 1099 consulting work for a smaller company that was partially owned by a very large corporation. The company began at a friend's kitchen table and grew to about one hundred people. I was hired because the company had no real experienced people supporting their most profitable product. When the large company infused capital into them, they could hire me.

About one and a half years into it, the people at the larger corporation began to believe they had purchased a good idea which wasn't really interested in being a successful company. In fact, some of the people at the smaller company were so bad at their main product (a loss leader), the CEO decided to stop selling it, which was about 85 percent of the company's activity.

The CEO had twenty-five people fired. The head attorney pulled me aside and said, "Chase, this doesn't apply to you. You will be laid off, too, but we don't have anyone else who knows what they're doing in your department, so we need you to work another month." And then I was fired.

Okay, no problem. But then the attorney asked me to work a second month—same problem. Well, guess what happened a month later? The very same thing! They asked me to stay another month, but this time the CEO personally asked me to stay for a third month.

About a week after that, I had to run something by the CEO. When I got to his office, he immediately said, "What are you doing here?" I replied, "I am doing such and such, and you asked me to work until the end of November." His response? "I never said that. Get out."

So, I had a job, then didn't. Had a job again, then didn't.

And then I had a job again, and then didn't, all in less than three months.

Do you know anyone who's been divorced and their whole identity either washes away or, worse yet, they stay in the "poor me" ego thing? Know anyone who has had a family member die and their whole personality changes to the "I'm sad about such and such person" ego thing? Sure, we all do. I have great empathy for these people—people that have faced or been in tragic situations. These are people who got knocked down seven times and never got up the eighth time. Staying on the floor means you lose. You've given up. Or, perhaps this was the first knock down they experienced, and they just did not have the drive (or sometimes, desire) to overcome and integrate.

There was a comic on TV a few years back who introduced herself something like this: "Hi, I am such and such. A little while ago I got fired from my job, my husband divorced me, my mom died, my house burned down, and then . . . I got cancer. That's when I started to laugh." She was hysterically funny! By getting back up on *her* feet, dusting *herself* off, she gave *us* permission to think *our* lives weren't so bad when sometimes we thought our lives were so bad. You just really cannot top her story. And that's kind of the point: There is always someone else who has it way worse than we do in our down moments, and they got back up and kicked butt in their life.

Remember that life's downturns aren't after us. They are not personal. They're after *everybody*. Nobody gets out of life alive!

YOUR ASSIGNMENT

People that don't get back up are *not* bad people, and they are *not* doing a bad thing. I'm not saying that at all. They are just not Mind Warriors.

What I am saying is you have a choice. If you stay

down or if you get back up that eighth time, no one is going to pin a medal on your chest or make you a movie star (maybe a TV and nightclub comic). And this includes being scared. How often has someone you know—or maybe even you—not done something that would help you, or they didn't get or be or have what they wanted, and didn't, because you or they were not comfortable with it?

When Ms. Kristin Andree, twenty years younger than me, landed a kick to the left side of my head in front of the whole martial-arts school, and I went down, what did I do? I got back up. (Okay, okay, at some point I would have had to get back up even if just to go home.) But when the head instructor asked me if I was okay and asked if I needed to sit out, I said, "I'm fine, sir. Just needed a moment," and I went back to sparring Ms. Andree. The rest of that match didn't fare any better for me, but by God I got better at blocking kicks from my left!

By the way, did I mention that if you are not getting knocked down every two or three years, you just aren't trying? This includes emotional knocks, physical, or life-situation setbacks. And guys, we have emotional knocks, too. Admit it—we just scream, yell, and break things rather than cry. (So, who's smarter with these? Yes, women.)

So, here is your homework. If nothing around you has knocked you down, look into your past and see if you did not "get back up the eighth time" at some point. See how you can address that today. Go ahead. I'm right here with you. And remember, if it's not scary, it's not good enough for you.

Write down your experiences and revisit what you wrote in two weeks' time.

Mind Warriors always get back up and keep fighting, because that's what we do.

Success happens when the prepared meet opportunity.

—NFL Coach Jimmy Johnson

Axiom 10 : Always Put Yourself into a Position to Win by Always Preparing to Be Ready

THE BACKGROUND

Mind Warriors are constantly forging their swords. As we strike the hot steel, it conforms to our vision. As we pound its shape, it conforms to our will. As we unsheathe it, others will know our wisdom. I saw a gentleman speak a few years ago about how he came to be a college basketball player on, I believe, the UNC team. He was, and may still be, an actor local to the Metro Atlanta area.

He was speaking to a luncheon of the Special Olympics

of Georgia. It was one of the most important talks I'd heard in a very long time. When this gentleman was in high school, perhaps earlier, he wanted to be a high school and college basketball player. But guess what? He didn't have the physical body for it, nor the skill, but he had desire and he saw nothing else.

Please pay special attention to this last point. His mind, in my view, never focused on all the reasons why he couldn't; his mind focused on just the things he could do to make his dream happen. And, it is also possible that if his mind focused on one of the many barriers to being a basketball player, he deftly stepped around them.

MY MESSAGE

So, what this gentleman did is this: everything he needed to do to become a strong basketball player. When his friends were running around playing after school, he did his homework and then practiced basketball in his driveway—endlessly.

He trained, and trained, and trained. He had his mind set on being a basketball player, reviewed where he would have to be physically, and created a plan to get from where he was to where he needed to be.

As it turns out, a few years later he was in a position where an opportunity opened up for him to . . . guess what? To be on the college basketball team! *But*, if he had not prepared (and prepared seriously) to be a college-level basketball player, when the door of opportunity opened up for him, he could not have stepped through. In other words, when his ship came in, he made sure he was at the dock.

Personal story: I sort of fell into writing my first published book. It came from a desire to answer common questions about a topic few corporate people really knew about (*Chasin' Meditation*). I really liked writing the book and didn't intend to do additional writing, but when a new chiropractor moved into town and wanted to write a book, she asked me to ghostwrite it for her at a very good fee. She knew her profession extremely well, but was not a writer.

No problem. Most people aren't there—yet. If I had not gone through the challenging work of writing a book before, I would not have been prepared to do so for someone else. And then that gig moved me to a second gig, and then a third, and then to this book.

Sometimes Mind Warriors may not know what we are preparing for—what might be over the horizon—until we do the work. It may take us by complete surprise, which adds extra fun to life.

YOUR ASSIGNMENT

Pick something you would *really* like to do. Maybe you want to captain a sailboat. Maybe you want to be an attorney. Maybe you want to have your MBA or PhD. Great. Let's call it your "near-term goal." It doesn't matter what it is, as long as it is a significant desire for you.

Your homework is to take a few days and research what you need to do to achieve that. Look at time, money, space, and the fact that some of your friends may change. (Some people will go along in your growth and some will not want to.) Map out what it would take—a mini–business plan, so to speak. You could do it on a paper napkin. Then ask yourself, "Am I interested enough in doing the activities and enduring the discomfort it requires to achieve my near-term goal? Am I willing to exchange other activities in order to achieve my near-term goal?"

You may find that the activity exchange required only involves how much time you spend on the couch drinking beer in front of the TV or having your nose glued to your telephone (yes, it's a telephone, not a magic miracle device).

Your next step is to share this dream with your dream team. Your dream team may be your closest friends, your children, your parents, people in your religious community, or past teachers. Ask them what they think.

Reassess. If the answer is yes, take the first steps.

Three weeks later, check in with yourself as to how you feel. If it's mostly fear or mostly excitement, charge on for three more weeks, then another three. After three to four months, take a pause, perhaps over a glass of wine, or a good craft beer, or a special scotch . . . I'm digressing. Simply see how you feel about your life at this three-to-four-month place as compared to when you first started. Share with others.

Write down your experiences and revisit what you wrote in two weeks' time.

Mind Warriors are constantly forging our swords.

As we strike the hot steel, it conforms to our vision. As we pound its shape, it conforms to our will. As we unsheathe it, others will know our wisdom.

HOW BLACK BELTS *persevere* DIFFERENTLY

Attitude is everything.

—Coach Jay Wright, Villanova Basketball

Axiom 11: A Black Belt Is a White Belt Who Never Quit

THE BACKGROUND

Mind Warriors never measure themselves by what another person has, or does, or is.

When a prospective student or parent comes into our school, and they say, "I'd like to sign up for Black Belt training. What does it take to become a Black Belt?", the answer is, "Yes, sir/ma'am, I'd be glad to help you with that. And let me start out by telling you that absolutely, you will achieve your Black Belt. **A Black Belt is a White Belt that never quit.** It *is* this simple. All you have to do is come to class as scheduled, learn the things we teach, practice outside of school, and attend the required testings. We will guide you each step of the way, and we will not ever let you fall behind."

Where this goes awry is when a person quits. And on average, about 90 percent will quit before testing for their Black Belt. In a very, very small percentage of instances, a student drops out of school because of health reasons (injury or illness), or sometimes for economic or other life situations that make it impossible. But, almost all who do drop from training do so because they *choose* not to train further. It might be because of how hard it can be. It might be because the stress of testing for your Black Belt is, well, stressful! It is almost always because **their mind lets them quit.**

Starting something meaningful is a choice. We grow by making strong choices and playing them out. When they don't work, we reassess, make a better choice, and keep going. When you stop exercising a strong, positive choice, other people increase their influence in your mind.

MY MESSAGE

Where this can also go awry is when a person starts to beat themselves up for not having or having done this or that by such and such age. Statistically, those that achieve extraordinary results early are few and far between—almost infinitesimal. Think about it. An extraordinary achievement at an extraordinarily young age is not "ordinary." Plus, life is structured to give you all sorts of opportunity to overcome challenges.

Hey, this can suck, I know. I could beat myself up all day long for waiting until I was fifty-four to sign up for Black Belt training, only to get kicked in the head each and every Tuesday night by Mr. Chalfant (a stronger, younger, much higher belt than me). This went on for two years. It would have been *a whole lot* better if I'd started at thirty-four instead of fifty-four, but I didn't. So what? I had to get over it and get over it fast.

I saw a great saying the other day. It went, "Life always

gives you a second chance. It's called tomorrow." So, don't give up because you simply didn't hit your target on the exact day and time you wanted to. Keep going.

In Western society, there is too much emphasis on achieving this or that by such and such age. We want to have a house by X age, be married by Y age, and have a child by Z age, let alone be a professional/corporate superstar or owner by, let's say, thirty-two years old. These are all fine and good. On the one hand, if we don't have plans and don't have targets, we are significantly less likely to hit/do/achieve what we want to do by this age or that age. But on the other hand, this can be a killer if we condemn ourselves for not hitting a target by X target date—an absolute killer. Remember, the first person to finish life is, well, dead! Why would you ever be in a rush to win that?

Where this goes well is when we see these occasional extraordinary achievers and we offer them love, respect, and excitement for their accomplishments—even more when they do it early in life. Better get over that. Get excited. Be thrilled. And then get back to *your* life.

In most societies, the recognition of a person's value directly increases with a person's age, and that makes sense. Wisdom can only come from experiences. Extreme wisdom can only come from the ability to survive great difficulty. Only older persons, respectfully known as elders, have the necessary experience for wisdom or extreme wisdom.

YOUR ASSIGNMENT

Make a list of five people who achieved extraordinary things when they were very young. (We'll be making more than just this list, so perhaps dedicate a notebook or pad for your Mind Warrior training.)

Then, make a list of five people who achieved

extraordinary things when they weren't very young. I'll give you a starting point: John Wayne. He didn't become a movie star until after over seventy movies, when he starred in the film *Stagecoach*. He appeared in over two hundred and fifty movies. He became so good and so highly respected that he couldn't walk into a room anywhere without everyone standing up and applauding.

Your homework: Now that you have your list, go through each person, name by name, and try to convince yourself that the list of "older people" were not just as successful or had just as meaningful lives as the "younger people" did.

Oh, and yeah, I know what you may be thinking. *What about this jerk or that jerk that gets promoted, paid more, wins the election, has a happier marriage, drives a better car than I do? I am so much more capable, and produce better work products, and am a better spouse than they will ever be. Justify that, Mr. Mind Warrior Chase Carey!*

My response is, I can't. I have ideas about why such things happen, and if I am correct, I cannot change them, you cannot change them, and they shouldn't be changed.

Write down your experiences and revisit what you wrote in two weeks' time.

Mind Warriors never measure themselves by what another person has, or does, or is.

I think we've lost touch with the value of failure and mistakes.

—Cheryl Bachelder, Interim CEO at Pier 1, Director at US Foods

Axiom 12: Losing Completely Is Often the Best Lesson

THE BACKGROUND

Mind Warriors know that losing completely is often the most powerful teacher. You may not have learned how to handle disappointment yet, but it's something you really need to experience. Does losing suck? Totally. But suck it up, buttercup, or forever be just one of the dogs in the back of the dogsled dog team (where the scenery never changes). Get it?

Let's take the second point first. The other day my wife and I were watching a talent-search TV show. One of the acts was a stand-up comic with a goofy hat, a long beard that got in the way, *and* he played an accordion! We thought the same thing you are: *What a completely stupid, outdated act. This guy needs to get eliminated right off the bat.* And, it wasn't long before the first judge voted for elimination.

At this point we are loving that judge, and knew this guy and his stupid act are soon to be off the stage. We were anticipating the boot. (A note of clarification: my wife and I are not your typical "throw that act off the stage" people; we admire all people that go out on a big limb. This guy was just so bad, we figured the producer was playing a joke on the judges.)

A couple of earlier acts had just been booted and the moment they got their elimination votes, they immediately left the stage. But not our buddy Mr. Accordion. With each and every elimination vote he got, he seamlessly shot back to the judges with a clever quip. After the third elimination vote (which was enough to get him *thrown* off the stage), he said something like this to the judges: "Geez, all these elimination votes are starting to affect my self-confidence," and he continued on.

My former martial-arts chief instructor, Master Burns, often shares with us that the difference between a new student and a master is the master has failed many more times than the new student has even tried. If you are not bruised, you are not yet ready to learn. A little bruising *can* be a good thing.

MY MESSAGE

Long story short, Mr. Accordion continued to banter with the judges. He didn't fight back. He *deflected* their criticism and bantered them into something, yet again, thought-provoking and clever. The judges finally gave in and came around. Why? Because they knew Mr. Accordion was right. He didn't shy away from defeat; he learned from it, deflected its wounds, and reengaged in a new and clever way. He knew how to entertain, and he knew how to recover from defeat.

Had he not failed completely on that stage, he would not have been so good. And he was good.

So, how do *you* deal with defeat? First off, know that very, very few people step up in the first place. My professional speaking coach, Dawn Andrews, says it this way: "Most people never walk onto the court/ playing field in the first place. So, when you've got the opportunity and decide to walk on, you've already won! We're just waiting on the score. If you choose to never walk on, you haven't earned the right to judge or critique those of us who do."

Dawn is telling us that if you try but don't win, you *do not* fail. You simply may not win that day. When Black Belts test for their next higher belt, if we do not pass the testing, we do not say we failed; we only say we did not earn a belt change that day.

You *always* win by exerting your will; it's just that many people get confused about the timeline involved with winning. Except for the few people that win with the first spin on a slot machine or their first lottery ticket, the rest us do not experience the world that way. Other than the two examples just mentioned, there is not an extremely successful person on the planet who "won" the very first time they tried something. In fact, if you ever studied overnight successes in the entertainment industry, almost all overnight success occurred *only* after years of brutal effort.

Let's move more corporate and talk about Cheryl Bachelder. Cheryl is interim CEO of Pier 1 and a director of US Foods, former CEO of Popeye's Louisiana Kitchen, president and chief concept officer at KFC US, a leadership author, and more. As an extremely talented and accomplished individual, we would tend to think, *Man, she had it going on*. And she did, but she also made mistakes larger than many of us will ever have the opportunity to make. That's because there is *nothing* Cheryl does small. She only does *big*.

Not too long ago, she was quoted in the *Hillsdale Collegian* about what it was like to fail (and to fail big time). She said, "I think we've lost touch with the value of failure and mistakes. Failure's a pretty strong word—let's just say mistakes. We don't learn very much from success. But, boy, lose a game in life or sports, and you review the tapes." And ain't that the God's given truth?

When we win, we don't always know why we win, particularly if the task or event was complex. What were the real drivers in success? People that have never failed really don't know. They only *think* they know. That doesn't mean don't listen to them, but it does mean hard experience is an incredibly powerful teacher, and if you can find someone with tough experiences, listen to what they have to say and test it dutifully.

It's hard to tell what the success drivers really are when you've never hit the floor hard. It's hard to tell what the success drivers really are if you haven't failed after doing everything right. It's really hard to tell if someone has the "right stuff" if they have never struggled and persevered (more on perseverance later).

Imagine if you looked at all your "mistakes" (thanks, Cheryl) as simply not getting the result you wanted *that* day. Imagine if you looked at the mistakes of others as a learning tool instead of a mess up. Imagine how that would enable you to lead more and lead more deeply.

People that are natural at winning may not really understand what aspects of their performance are being measured aside from the obvious things, like winning a race or eating the most hotdogs. (I am seriously concerned about people who partake in food-eating contests.) I was a good combat sparrer as a Color Belt and not too bad as a Black Belt. In one match, I lost horribly to a guy that was only average at best. But I lost ten to zero, which was *losing completely*! Ouch! And, I did this in front of my big brother, a big-time federal judge, the first time I invited anybody to watch me compete. What a disappointment.

I was embarrassed, so it was a very good test to set aside the ego for me, which got me thinking. Were the judges incompetent? No. Were the judges bad people? Again, no. So, I met with my instructor, and he helped me hash out not where I went wrong, but where my strikes were not counted. We then made a plan to make sure they were counted, and guess what? I got back to winning and placing.

Here's the secret: Once I "sucked up my buttercup" and moved on, I learned that the judges don't see every hit because combat sparring is so fast. I learned to control my opponent's body position so the judges were more likely to see my strikes. I also learned to keep striking my opponent until the judges shouted, "Point!"

You see, what I had been doing was relaxing my weapon and pulling back once I struck, expecting to earn a point. But while I was relaxing from a strike the judges did not see, my opponent was still in striking mode, and that's all the judges saw. How can such a lesson work in your life? At work? At home? In your community?

Ask yourself, would you rather be a Black Belt who lost a competition, or a no-belt that has never lost at anything because you never tried at anything? My vote goes to person A.

YOUR ASSIGNMENT

Pick something and lose at it. If you are already engaged in one or more activities that take quite a bit of learning and practice, compete early or speak on the subject early. Don't intentionally screw it up; that's not the same thing. Go after something you are *not* prepared to do, and do it.

This can also mean if you play in a golf, tennis, or even jousting league (we have one of those eat-with-your-hands Medieval restaurants near us), decide to compete at a higher level and see how you do. When you don't win (remember, you can't lose if you sincerely try), play the tapes and see where you did not perform at the level required to win, and work like hell practicing the better movement.

Write down your experiences and revisit what you wrote in two weeks' time.

Mind Warriors know that losing completely is often our most powerful teacher.

Axiom 13: If You Ain't Cryin', You Ain't Tryin'!

THE BACKGROUND

Mind Warriors know the more we sweat today, the cooler we will be tomorrow. One of my favorite martial-arts instructors, Mr. Johnathan Chapovsky, fourth-degree Black Belt, says this all the time. He generally says it about the time all of us in class start to moan due to the workout prior to the actual training. He just smiles and says, "You know what I say—if you ain't cryin', you ain't tryin'!" And it's a very, very good point.

It also hits us psychologically, because it reinforces to us that there *is* an end game to what we are doing. We are not just doing something to keep us off the couch.

There's also a great saying used by the US Navy SEALs and others that goes something like this: "Sweat today or bleed tomorrow." (It's unlikely that bleeding is in your future, but you get the idea.)

MY MESSAGE

It's not always—and does not have to be—physical pain that gets you crying. Sometimes, particularly as an adult, it is very, very difficult to grow without some level of emotional challenge. The more and the faster you want to grow, the more severe the struggle. Yes, it's just sort of this way.

Most all of the people we see who are living their dream have endured—or are enduring—significant struggles. They chose to exchange comfort for achievement of their desires. Most overnight success came only after a lot of blood, sweat, and tears.

People from Sylvester Stallone to Tyler Perry have had

Give me twenty more, Mr. Carey!

—Mr. Jonathan Chapovsky, Fourth-Degree Black Belt

Only twenty, sir?

—C. Chase Carey

Make it fifty!

—Mr. Jonathan Chapovsky, Fourth-Degree Black Belt

significant struggles. Sylvester Stallone had to sell his wife's jewelry (it turns out that was a *really bad idea*) and even sell his *dog* because he could no longer afford to feed it (see Axiom 15). Tyler Perry opened his first the-atrical performance to a mostly empty theater because it was the July 4 holiday in Atlanta; everyone was out doing something else. This caused him to end up living out of his car. Today, he flies a beautiful, very large Gulfstream, which I've seen from the outside. (HINT: Mr. Perry, I'd love to see it from the inside!)

Mind Warriors know the higher we go, the thinner the air, the faster the flight. All we need to do to get started is to reach.

YOUR ASSIGNMENT

Have a breakdown—a good one.

Need an example close to home? Sure, here's one. A person I've trained with, Sandra, recently left her (very) good corporate job in uncomfortable circumstances. She decided to sell her house in Metro Atlanta, move to Costa Rica, buy a house there, and start a yoga studio in a major residential-hotel-business development. Oh, and by the way, she wasn't even a certified yoga teacher at this point.

She did plan on taking her husband with her, settling on just one income instead of two. It had taken her, her husband, and the developer hundreds of hours of negotiations and details. Phew, finally all of the details were worked out, so she and her husband flew to Europe for a beautiful European vacation, kind of a "last hurrah" after her difficult corporate experience. She broke her leg falling down at an historic site in Rome. When you fly coach, that's a tall order.

From there, they flew to Costa Rica, broken leg and all, checked over all the many details to make sure all her ducks were in a row, including their ability to live and work in the country lawfully, and sat down at a big table with lots of lawyers to sign the enormous stacks of paper to make it all happen.

At home outside Atlanta, her Realtor was literally at the very moment setting up a drone to take house pics. As Sandra reached for her pen, she lost it. Total meltdown. And I mean total: crying, panicking, incoherent statements. The lawyers were in shock and could not understand what she was doing and why. She rose from the table, excused herself, turned back to her husband and said, "Are you coming?!" She called her Realtor, told her not to sell the house, boarded a plane, and flew back to the States.

Game over. Done.

So, you might be asking, "Where's the benefit? Where's the big result? Where's the great 'thing' that came out of it?" **Breakdowns deliver value by creating breakthroughs. A breakthrough is a quantum leap to a new level of understanding, skill, and power.** All breakthroughs create a newer, more effective version of yourself. And after all, this is what being a Mind Warrior is *all* about.

I saw Sandra in class just a week later, and she was as together as any human being ever was. She had a very big test that day, and she aced it like child's play. It was simply not possible for her to have done a more perfect job than she had done that day. I truly believe if she had not had the meltdown in Costa Rica, she wouldn't have been nearly as confident.

Sandra's breakdown brought her great confidence. With great confidence, a person can do anything. I heard from her recently, and she and her husband were back to traveling and having the best time of their lives. Her breakdown was one of the best things that ever happened to her.

At some point, and some point relatively soon after you have your first minimeltdown, should you push the envelope that hard, the meltdown will go away completely. But until then, if you are not having at least one minimeltdown every few years, you are pretty much standing still. And that's okay, if that's your thing.

Write down your experiences and revisit what you wrote in two weeks' time.

Mind Warriors know the more we sweat today, the cooler we will be tomorrow.

Axiom 14: You Get What You Get!

THE BACKGROUND

Mind Warriors demonstrate to others that "we get what we get," and we are just not going to let "bad" things stop us or redefine us.

During my first-degree Black Belt preparation, we had an additional four Saturdays outside in the elements where we ran, did pushups, sit-ups, all sorts of exercises, and practiced our forms (barefooted). The first Saturday morning it was twenty-eight degrees outside, and it sucked. Nobody was happy, particularly when we found out the schools on the other side of town had taken their practice to the warm, dry inside of their facilities.

Suck it up, buttercup!

—What my wife says to me when I don't get what I want

During a normally scheduled practice, a testing student who had not made it to the outside run the weekend before asked our chief instructor, "What happens if it rains, or it's cold [on the morning of testing]?"

Master Burns actually stopped class, looked at the student, and said: "You—get—what—you—get!" Then, Master Burns chuckled and went on to explain to the student that he was testing for his first-degree Black Belt. The student had been training for three years straight at least three nights a week, maybe—tournaments, memorizations, maybe private lessons—all while doing his school assignments on time, athletics at school, doing his chores, and paying attention to his parents. Was he, the student, going to let a little cold rain stop him?

The answer came back as a very strong "No!"

MY MESSAGE

Let's start with a great quote by Mark Twain: "The two

most important days in your life are the day you are born and the day you find out why." Maybe that's why we get what we get!

The true test is how you deal with real challenges. How do you deal with unexpected death? How do you deal with divorce, expected or not? How do you deal with significant illnesses of you or your spouse, or God forbid, one of your children? How do you deal with not getting that once-in-a-lifetime promotion? How do you deal with a house fire? How do you deal with a significant car accident?

When I worked in corporate America and was in a position to hire someone, I always looked for someone who did not move through life with only a silver spoon. For younger applicants, if I came to know that they worked their way through school, that was a big plus. If they always had summer jobs, the harder the better, that was a plus. A veteran? He or she got additional points above those prescribed by law.

I remember one veteran I hired. On his very first day, before training even began, I gave him a quote to run. Two hours later, he popped by my office and said, "Just interrupting to let you know the quote is done and out. I know you are busy. Bye." He, at the time, happened to be going through a very nasty divorce and other legal challenges. Do you understand how he was able to do the work with zero training? Focus. All he thought about was, *How do I get this done, and get it done well and on time?* And then he took the right steps to do that, nothing else, and never entertained the thoughts of excuses like, *What? Why me? This is my first day!*

God, I love working with vets.

YOUR ASSIGNMENT

Consider each of these "bad" things that could possibly have happened to you or perhaps others. Or, if you've experienced one or more of these challenges, think back on how you survived.

Mind Warriors do much more than just survive—we thrive! We move through the challenge, integrate it, and move forward. Trust me, once you've successfully moved through and beyond one of these challenges, you will be a much better person. It does take guts.

Some people never move beyond just surviving such challenges, becoming frozen in time. You may have met or know such people by the way you learn about them, such as, "Oh yeah, that's Devon from finance. His dad died of cancer." Maybe it's "That's Stephanie from marketing. She had her two-year-old son die in a car crash ten years ago." These fictitious examples and extreme challenges point out that many of us can go from being Devon, to Devon whose mom died; from Stephanie, to Stephanie whose child died ten years ago.

Thrive by understanding that "bad" things happen to most people; that if you do not attach an unhelpful meaning to a tragic event, do the very best you can to find love in your learning from that event, and don't wear it around your neck like an anchor for all to see; that life *does* go on.

Write down your experiences and revisit what you wrote in two weeks' time.

Mind Warriors demonstrate to others that "we get what we get," and we are just not going to let bad things stop us *or* define us.

I've missed more than nine thousand shots in my career. I've lost almost three hundred games. Twenty-six times, I've been trusted to take the game-winning shot and missed. I've failed over, and over, and over again in my life. And that is why I succeed.

—Michael Jordan

Axiom 15: Persistence and Perseverance—A Lesson from Sylvester Stallone

THE BACKGROUND

Mind Warriors are all Rockys, even when we slip. Persistence is (one of) the most powerful exercises of will a person can do. Exercising will is one of the most powerful creative sources a person has available to them. (Do *not* underestimate the force in this last sentence. It is likely the most powerful concept in this entire book.)

MY MESSAGE

At a Tony Robbins fire-walk workshop in Tampa, Mr.

Robbins spoke of Sylvester Stallone's story about getting his film *Rocky* made. It's an incredible story about perseverance and focus. I'll apologize right up front and say I may not remember all the details correctly, but I do not know Mr. Stallone to pick up the phone and call him. The exact details aren't the lesson—it's his laser focus of his mind and body that counts.

Here's the story: Sylvester Stallone wrote the screenplay for *Rocky*. A great story and great screenplay, but he just could not get anyone to make the movie with him starring in it. (How would you like to be one of the many people who turned him down?) After a while, he did get offers for just the screenplay, but there was no way in hell an unheard-of actor was going to play the main role in the movie. But, Sylvester wouldn't sell it without him starring in it.

So, life went on, but Sylvester didn't have a job. So, one day he sold his wife's jewelry. Sylvester told Tony, "Never sell your wife's jewelry." Apparently it was a pretty big mistake, so guys, don't sell your wife's jewelry. (Ladies, it's probably okay to sell your husband's jewelry, but do so very carefully.)

In their shitty apartment in New York City, times and money got harder and harder. In fact, it got so bad, Sylvester could no longer feed his dog, took him down to a street corner, and found someone to buy his dog from him. You know that had to completely suck for him and his wife. There is just nothing worse than *not* being able to care for someone or a pet you are responsible for.

Eventually, Sylvester found someone to buy the script from him for, I think, about $500,000 (a lot of money then). Again, the exact number is not important, but Mr. Stallone continued to insist that he star in the film. This argument with the potential buyer apparently went on for a very long time. Eventually the buyer capitulated and agreed to have Sylvester in the film, but he slashed the price he was willing to pay to $100,000. Sylvester took it—amazingly great news for Sylvester and his wife.

Sylvester was so relieved, he went back out to that street corner where he sold his dog to buy him back. It took several nights until the man who had bought his dog came by one evening, dog in tow. Sylvester immediately approached the man and said he wanted to buy his dog back because he had money now. The man replied by saying no, the dog no longer belonged to Sylvester; it belonged to him and was *his* dog. Sylvester persisted, and eventually the shrewd New Yorker asked how it was Sylvester all of a sudden had enough money to buy his dog back. Mistake or not, Sylvester told the man his story.

Well, before you know it, Sylvester did get his dog back, but at the price of $50,000 and giving the man a role in *Rocky*.

YOUR ASSIGNMENT

Google "the + founder + persistence," and watch the one-minute-and-twenty-three-second scene where the character played by Michael Keaton is in a motel room. The character listens to a motivational talk about persistence and determination. (Set aside, for the purposes of this exercise, that the character Michael Keaton plays in the movie was portrayed as a less-than-nice or honest person.)

Pay close attention to the comments about the masses of talented, bright, educated people who are not successful. (Trust me, these traits can be extremely helpful in life, but persistence can make up for a whole lot of these things missing.)

Is there something you would like to do, have, or perhaps be, that you have either not started to go after or have gone after without success (yet)? Ask yourself, **"What's my *Rocky*?"** It could be a promotion, a child, a nicer house, world travel, or a nicer lawn. What it is does not matter to me. It only has to matter to you.

Once you've found your *Rocky*, write out your persistence plan of attack, and then implement the plan.

Start today, tomorrow, or on Sunday or Monday. I like to start in the beginning of the week for no particular reason other than convenience.

Perhaps you want to write a book. Start out with a title and a table of contents. Then, in a week or two, create a very brief outline for chapter one. In week three, create a very brief outline for chapter two, and so forth.

Do you want to finish up your undergraduate degree? Check with HR to see what your company's tuition-reimbursement plan is, then start researching nearby schools.

Want a nicer house? Scour the real-estate listings online and find the area, the type of home, and price point that you are shooting for. (Be sure to estimate how your target area will change, if at all, five years after your target purchase date.) Maybe talk with an accountant, financial planner, a friend with a business background, or to your boss—someone who knows about owning the type of home you are targeting.

And maybe, just maybe, your *Rocky* is spending two more hours a week with your family, or in self-care and meditation for yourself (you knew I was going to throw in meditation), and begin.

Begin. Persist. Don't stop. When you slip up, care not and start again. Remember, most all people who have stopped an addictive behavior, like smoking, failed at their plan of not being addicted, but started again and did not beat themselves up for it.

Write down your experiences and revisit what you wrote in two weeks' time.

Mind Warriors are all Rockys. We never give up!

Be the change you wish
to see in the world.

—Ghandi

CALL TO ACTION

by John "JD" Dammann
Market Vice President, Wellness Leader, Humana

Look, folks, here's the thing: do the next right thing.

These Axioms give you plenty to choose from. What I've found over the years in leading sales teams is the number-one thing keeping good people from taking right action is that they are afraid that the next action they take won't be the "right" action. Trust me, whether or not the next action they take produces the result they want or gets them to the next action or set of actions that will—it doesn't matter. What matters is *forward movement.*

Let me say that again: it *doesn't matter* whether or not the next action you take produces the result you want or gets you to the action or actions that will. What matters is *forward movement.* These Axioms create forward movement in your life.

Take Axiom 9: "If you fall down seven times, get up eight." Keep going, keep moving. It doesn't matter how many times you've fallen down. Some of the best sales professionals I know have fallen down way more times than they remember. True, some only fall a few times, but that's rare. If you want to go for the big win in life—whatever that may be (family, friendships, finances, your pilot's license)—just keep going.

Axiom 10—"Always put yourself in a position to win by always preparing to be ready"—can be done by all the learning you may do as you fall down. It can also take as little as fifteen minutes a day. Don't like reading? Fine. Watch YouTube. There is so much advice for the taking just from there alone that I'll bet you could learn a PhD's level of knowledge in a relatively short period of time.

Here's a secret. Find the topic that lights your fire, then study and practice it in a disciplined manner. In a year, you will be one of the country's leading experts. In three years, you will have achieved a Black Belt's level of skill.

Let's not forget my favorite Axiom, Axiom 4: "Limit the access people have to you and your time." Boy, I just cannot say this enough. Not only are other people and things trying to steal your attention (not necessarily through bad intent), they are also trying to steal your mind. And you know what? Your mind is just fine the way it is (so long as you live one or more of the Axioms). Your mind *needs* downtime to re-grow and generate new ideas. There's an old military saying: "Why do generals have tents? They need to think." Create your own tent, and meditate in it. Then take action.

Which Axiom should you start with? The one that gets you excited, the one that gets you scared, or the first one? It doesn't really matter. And, after you've tried one out for five weeks, ask your team members or close friends to support your work with it and to pick out ones for themselves.

Go ahead. Go kick some real butt in life. Be a Mind Warrior.

Mind Warriors always take the next right action, whether or not it produces the result we want or it gets us to the action or actions that will. We know that what matters is forward movement!

ABOUT THE AUTHOR

C. Chase Carey, MBA, third-degree Black Belt, spent twenty years in corporate America's health insurance and consulting industry in significant positions, rising to vice president of underwriting for Aetna in the Southeastern US. He was then laid off, became self-employed as a consultant, an insurance broker, an author, a third-degree Black Belt in Tae Kwon Do, a corporate trainer in mindfulness and meditation, a yoga teacher, and now as a motivational speaker. He believes most of us can benefit greatly by learning the ways martial artists think and act differently from most people—without ever stepping into a martial-arts school.

Chase guest lectures at the Villanova School of Business and the Georgia campus of the Philadelphia College of Osteopathic Medicine. You can reach Chase and check out this and other trainings and speaking by Chase at www.ChasingMindfulness.com.

OTHER BOOKS BY
C. CHASE CAREY, MBA

Chasin' Meditation